INSIDE OUT HEART

Volume 1: Poems for my dying father & after

SJP Dooley

Copyright © 2020 by SJP Dooley

All rights reserved.

No part of this book may be reproduced in any form or any means, including information storage and retrieval systems, without the author's written permission, except brief quotations in a book review.

Volume 1 Ebook ISBN: 978-1-922399-01-4

Volume 1 Paperback ISBN: 978-1-922399-00-7

Volume 1 Audiobook ISBN: 978-1-922399-03-8

www.stellarviolets.org

A catalogue record for this work is available from the National Library of Australia

Published by Stellar Violets

For Peter Stanley Lees Dooley

&

for all of us who are living with dying

FOREWORD & POEM BY NIEL VAUGHAN

Poetry, for me, is a spiritual experience.

It never fails to astonish when something so complex and ethereal comes through the fingers and onto the page alive and fully formed.

It's a process of feelings and reactions.

I take a drink to invoke the spirits. Find a comfy couch and then begin to read you, your history, your poetry, your inner world. It's intimate and sad in that delightful way we enjoy Greek tragedies.

When my eyes begin to swim it's time for a dip in the subconscious; cool moss underfoot as the shadow self enters the inner deep;

the inner self detaches from the senses; a flash of lightning on the horizon; then, the rumble shudders and your poem arrives.

Witness the Witness

His father is preparing for what's coming next
    while he channels the path into text

The son witnessing the father slipping in-between
    into the place no living eye has ever seen

The brutal order of the living process
    a well-worn hand leaving his face with a gentle caress

And in these pages that follow
    lies a charted path into a dawning tomorrow

    For Simon

Niel Vaughan, Castlemaine 2020

THE ORIGINAL FALLEN GIANT
(FACING THIS ALONE)

A giant has fallen across my path
and now I don't know how to get through,
or what to do,
so I write this,
moved to irrelevance
as I contemplate
the size and force of this monolithic impediment.
And, so I begin to crawl across,
to go over and continue along the path.
But the grunting sounds repel me
beneath the giant,
back down the track,
down,
deeper into the forest.

Words

Words are useful, but only when nothing else will suffice.

IN WE LOVE MARGARET RESERVE

In We Love Margaret Reserve
We are supported
By a chair
And warm blanket to
Comfort you
From the biting cold
As you ease yourself
Into your chair
Bathe in warm sun's rays
Blinding even
Take the fruit
And
breakfast upon it
To help you on your long day's journey
Take some more
You'll need it Son
And, yes
It's like a treasure trove
For you

A playground
As you know
As he said
You're not alone
We are supported
This is home
I call to you
I love you Son
You know that
Tears
For each one
Don't let this go
You know
This rock
He has supported
But needs your help
We are supported
In this place
Allow yourself
Release the pace
Allow yourself
Feel the space
Allow yourself
Heart's embrace
Allow yourself
Sweet the taste
You have the time
Now look around
Come over here
Hear the sound
Of this bee
Coming for me
Sweet scent of rose

Of being home
Allow yourself
To feel this place
This my Son
My love's embrace

LATER IN WE LOVE MARGARET RESERVE

Later in We Love Margaret Reserve
This water backed up
(Possibly for years)
Comes forth
At first a trickle
Rivulets flow
Moisture
Staining the barren rock
Filtered by sand
Wind whipping leaves
The tempest builds
This water
Having now emerged from the depths
Reflects this Sun
Shimmers in this wind
Mirrors this place
Like a dog gnawing a boney stick
And running
In circles
Impossible to apprehend

You released this water
You did this
You always could
You just
Did not know it
Now you know
Pick up your stick
Your bone
And go
Run
Run
You cannot be caught
You are that wind
And you are running
And cannot be apprehended

LAND OF FORGOTTEN DREAMING

I'm letting the land wash over me
as we press on.
Ever onward
into this land of forgotten dreaming.
Images,
real,
come forth unbidden.
Passing out of sight before comprehension.
A calf rises to her mother's call.
The track,
fenced off.
Impassable.
A tiny track
spearing off.
Intimidating,
cutting off,
verging out,
and merging in.

2 FLIES CAUGHT IN A WEB

2 flies caught in a web
A larger blacker form emerges
Grabs one
A ferocious buzzing
It's still alive
Scooped up
Bundled
Rapidly carried into the lair
Stillness
Until the second fly moves
A larger blacker form swoops
And they are gone

CAGE-STRUCK

I am stuck
Inside this cage
Terrified
I screech
And flap
Interred
Within this trap
While you
My love
Flap
Like a mirror
Before me
And you are seen
And I am heard
The helper comes
To get me out
I flap and screech
His calm hands enveloping
I am whisked into the light

Freedom
Reunited
We fly to the highest branch

NUYTSIA FLORIBUNDA

Nuytsia floribunda are out.
WA Xmas trees.
Pangs of regret at leaving this place, at this time, for so long.
What am I doing?
And why?
I'm going to see Nicola and it is worth it.
It's a long trip.
Wondering whether Dad will ever see WA again?
Perhaps not...
What is going on?
I don't know.
The light blue sky and bright light is all pervasive.
Everything is so bright and tinged with a yellow hue.

GARETH

The gate fixed shut
when finally I arrive.
Wrenching, struggling,
sneaking beneath creepers,
crushed geranium wafting.
Crashing
onto my path
after all this time.
The youthful old gum
whose trunk stained with tears
now reflects this Summer's Sun.
And I am home
upon this path
after years.
Cutting meaninglessly
along the gumboot creek,
we walk that path forever
Gareth.

UNUSED TICKET

*He's unlikely to return
to this bush
he owns
but never really walked,
preferring roses
and lawn.
Dried branches snap.
He loved his view.
He loves his view.
Everyone does.
But I am taken
here.
Past the sewerage pipe.
Down,
down,
the mysterious
bubbling,
and holes for snakes.
The mystery sounds.*

Unseen
I know it.

FOREST SENTINEL

A rainbow
In the forest
Sentinel
Maintains this place
For us
Our feathers yet wet
Looking out
Readying ourselves
For the time to fly

ONE SQUARE FOOT

On this one square foot
    On which I stand
    I am
    Completely
    Here
    And
    Memories
    Exist
    But
    Do not
    Hold me
    Alone
    I walk
    Aware
    I walk
    Knowing
    I walk
    Standing
    I stand

Knowing
I stand

4:39AM (ON THE FIRST DAY OF YOUR LAST YEAR ON EARTH)

I like to feel the cold embrace of the morning air
As it freshens and wakens me
Calling forth a new day
A new year even
Cool
Refreshing
Beckoning
Calming
Soothing
Healing
Rewarding
Enabling
Beginning
Anew

THOSE TOO HEAVY SOUNDS

The ocean is so loud in my left ear
I can hardly hear myself think.
The right feels like an open vacuum with birds occasionally calling.
That sound of the ocean rumbling like that and crashing so loud in my left ear,
while my right ear is shielded from that.
Those too heavy sounds are not peaceful.
They are loud and overbearing,
but the soft sand is so soft,
and the soft water is sweet to my feet.
And so
I continue walking along this shore
in spite of that raucous sound.

HELD BY YOU (3RD AND FINAL OP)

Blue
Iridescent
Welcome
You hold me
I am you
Resting on the flexing bough
By the trickling stream
Far from the traffic
In this our home
Floating free
You welcome me
Here
In your ease calming
Holding me
In arrest
As darkness descends
Your iridescence continues to shine
You are not swayed by this night
You are the blue butterfly
Home

In this Jurassic world
Where nothing can retain you
An embodied spirit of this place
We hold each other
Free
Together
We are both transformed
Free together
We rise and fall
Free together
We sit
And listen
Trickling stream
Caws of crows
Cicadas a ton
Rumbling plane
And we sit
Together
We are free
And I am so grateful for our meeting
I walk on with you
Together
In freedom
Thank you
And
Goodnight

LIQUID HEART

Night scents fill the air
White petals fall
The last remaining rose of summer
Into the darkness I walk alone
Shining lights behind me
Darkness fills my vision
My heart liquid
I walk
Into the night

AT ALICE ROBINSON RESERVE 2 APRIL

Dad and Lucy came here all the time.
And Mum lived there.
Now they are all gone and only we are left.
And yet I can still see Nicola and Dad and Lucy there at the swings and the seats.
But that time has gone.
And only I am left.
Nicola is with her boyfriend, Pat.
And Dad is struggling with many things including his loneliness, at Gracewood Retirement Village.
And it's all painful.
And sorrowful.
And hard work.
And such loss.
Such loss.
Dad, who so easily walked up to this small park, will no longer be walking up here again.
And it's so sad and upsetting.
And I really don't know what to do.
Because there isn't anything I can do.

It is all past.

So I stop, and I smell the white rose at Jim the Roseman's place, the one that gives me the feeling of drinking fresh lemonade.

∼

"A monarch butterfly *came and just lightly touched my heart and flittered away*"

∼

LAND OF SADNESS, LONGING

There's something so sad about this landscape
So dry
So barren
So wasted
Such a wasteland
Waterless
It's marked by water
Absent of colour
It emphasises the blue sky
Sepia toned ink blots
Dried
Empty
Rectilinear
Sun faded
Bleached
A faded, colourless
Flat expanse
With oval salt pans

FLYING BACK TO DAD

Lights glimmer,
dazzling
as our torch rises
yet again.
Again, and again, and again.
In awe,
in wonder.
Airport waking up,
turbines whirring,
daylight emerging.
People mobbing
to this place
of arrivals
& departures.
The one celebrated,
the other mourned
in these tough times,
as they've always been.
Airbus A330 – 200

clomping like cloven hooves
our Virgin
Aircrew herd along the hard tiles;
"How's your Mum?"
"Yeah she's good."
Looks like it'll be the emptiest flight since 23 January & I
remember 2 years ago when
things were different
and
Dad was undiagnosed.
April 2017
& Nic & Carolyn shut down & I
Couldn't get Nic
& Dad, who was well then, & I
drove around
Galston
trying to get Nic
unsuccessfully,
& in 2 years time
he will have been gone some time
& that's
unbearably sad
as the night
is gone
and
heralded by
pink, blue
pastel hues
morning is
ours.
Korean Air with a Pepsi logo.
Jetstar
& our A330 – 200

awaiting.
Being packed &
readied.
Are we ever ready?
I am here for you Nic, just as Pa
has been for me!

TO BE AWARE

The idea is to be aware.
Painfully, and,
Ruthlessly
AWARE!
Living fully
Through the senses.
Experiencing it all.
Being & remaining
Open.
To experience.
To truth.
To connection.
She.
Her.
Her.
She moves me
In ways I have
Never understood,
But that my mother
Had an inkling of.

I continue to be moved
& confused & bewildered
& hurt & upset &
Embarrassed & opened
Up.
I feel the river of life
Lifting me
Up & off the
Muddy surface
& racing me
Along within
Its torrent
Bumping, colliding
With others in
Life & then away again.

DRIVING

One of my enduring memories of Dad, is of him driving.
Driving,
Always driving.
Driving our family,
Like Clark Griswold,
On trips
Up and down
The coast & to
Queensland.
Driving us in the
Dark
As I sat in the back dreaming
Of the girl I loved,
Listening to Go West's
The King of Wishful Thinking,
Or
Was it,
We Close Our Eyes?
As he drove himself &
His 3 sons

For a hospital visit
To his wife at
St John of God, Richmond.
Or
Was it
Windsor, or Richmond?
He loved driving &
Had many stories of
Driving old Austin A40s
Without windscreen
Wipers or heaters.

SOMEWHERE

Somewhere over the
Southern Ocean
The white caps
Of that frigid
Sea
Whip up
Beneath the sunny
Blue sky

I ASK THE BIRDS IN THE SKY, "HOW AM I GOING TO COPE WITH ALL OF THIS?"

How am I going to cope with all of this?

I'm asking you for help Gareth,
asking for help from the universe.

Asking for help from the spirits,
from everybody,
from friends,
from family,
from animals and plants,
from the sticks and stones,
from all there is,
in the trees,
in the sky,
and the sun, especially the sun,
and all of the beings, unseen and alive.

Find the joy, find the joy, find the joy.

Sit with the pain.

Walk, walk, walk.

Murmuration of the birds,
murmuration of the birds,
these birds
coming into the light,
into the light,
into the light,
into the black,
then the white,
and then turning back,
turning above me,
white birds fluttering,
fluttering, fluttering,
then black birds,
and white again,
and then gone.

Only to return again on the next circling.

Circling birds
catching the morning light.
Circling birds catching the morning sun.
Birds.
Birds.
40 or more birds circling together as one.
Free within the space of space.
As one they become dark and continue to circle, and as they circle
as one they become white against blue sky
as they continue to circle.
They continue to circle into the light,
and into the dark,
into the light,

and into the dark,
into the light again,
a circling manifestation of existence
into the light,
circling into the dark,
circling into the light,
circling in the dark
always beautiful,
always in motion,
always Life.
And they have no great awareness
of their circling into the light,
and into the dark,
into the light,
and into the dark.

They simply are.

The birds.
The birds circling into the light,
and into the dark,
into the light,
into the dark.
I see them circling
and circling
in continual momentum
as the birds circle
into the light,
into the dark,
and into the light,
and into the dark,
and into the light,
into the dark,

the birds in the sky.

OVER ROOKWOOD

Previously Dad's death was a theoretical eventuality.
Now it is a pressing imminent reality.
It's emotional and somber.
This trip
of ascension.
Remembering that Icarus flew too close to the Sun.
Out of balance.
Fly,
and be aware.
We flew over Rookwood cemetery.
I miss Jervis trips with Nic.
The beauty of the snaking river astounds me.
It slowly expands out to a lake.
It is organic.
Its fissures like ink on blotting paper
disappearing into the mist.
It is
so lovely.
I miss it

even as I'm taken
by the blue sky.

HIS PAIN

I can't think straight in here
It's driving me insane
Draining the blood from my bones
Let me out of here
Let me go
Let me outta my Kellyville cage
But no
I remain
Trapped
And alone

DEAR ROSE

Part I

Dear rose
We have travelled
So far
To weep
Together
Dear rose
Intoxicant
That your perfume is
I
Can not inhale enough of you
Nuzzled in
To you
Only song birds witness
Our coming together
And even they do not know

Part II

And so
At the end of it all
I return to you dear rose
Your scent ever same
Even as your flowers shift and age
And wither
Only to be replaced
By new shoots
And flowers
Your scent unwavering
Calling forth
For more

DAD IS DYING

Dad is dying
He has no will to live
Consider this
His life
Ending
Over
Going
From this body that is failing him
Just as he has been failed
Allow him
Space
Be there
Find your own peace
Find your own zen and be that

BEING RELEASED

~

I have to see this as you being released
Simply released
Naught else
Simply seeing you released
Anything else is not correct
An illusion

~

MIRROR NOIR

Waking up in the darkness
Mysterious
Black window
Like a black mirror
Revealing nothing
Though everything is there

THE CANAL'S EDGE

Just past the bridge where the muddied bike lays,
there's a path that disappears
where the holly grows,
but if you keep walking, one step after the other will
*   take you down stairs to a jetty*
whereupon you will gaze
at the mother and her ducklings and listen to the
*   sounds of the morning birds*
and the passing tram bell.
This is what you will do when your father is dying
and you've done all you can.

THE TRUTH

Dad's body is failing him now.
It happens to all of us.
It's an unbearably bitter pill to swallow.
And we choke, and gag on it.
But the truth is that his body is no longer the capable
　　vehicle that it's been for him all his life, that has
　　faithfully served him in so many ways
and, so, he is to be released.
Released from his pain and suffering.
And we mourn his pain,
and his loss,
and our loss.
But we are comforted to know that he had a good life.
That he needed relief,
and the relief he needed was granted him.
This is a comfort,
his finding peace.

UNTIL NOW

Burnished glow
Rippling toward me
Just as she came
Once
And visited me
Here
As you did
We did
Together
Countless times
But never stopping
Until
Now

NEW FORMS

These shells are new.
Formed in recent years.
They're made up of stuff;
sand, and aggregates
that were here when I used to come here.
But they are new.
New forms.
And that is the thing
with this death thing.
Yes, the old forms go
but new forms come.
And are the new not beautiful too?

REVEALING GLORY

And there they are again.
The flock of light and shade birds,
as they flutter into the light reflecting whiteness.

Shining bright,

then shifting, turning away from the light.

Becoming shadows of themselves.

Dark and stark against the brightness of the morning
   sky.

The light and the dark in the one.

The one in the many.

The many forming the one,

but not taking away from

the individuality of the one within the many.

But it is the many that reveal the glory of the flock.

GO

Go.
Let it all go.
Don't waste another moment on any of it.
Relax.

Be.

Feel yourself breathing.
Your blood flowing effortlessly.

You are in this moment, walking on this land that is supporting you.

This is enough.

Continue in joy.

Be cool.

Be whole.

Be whole.

Be whole.
Be whole.
Be whole.
Be whole.

You are within the whole.

Relax.
Go with it.

Look around and see.

And you will see that you lie within your form, and you will see all the forms around you, and you will see all of the forms around you of which your body is one.

And it is nothing to hold onto it, so let it go.

Feel your breath inside you, as your comet is inside you, all good and whole and healthy.

Traumatic moments come and go and you continue on.

Your Comet continues on.

Your Comet continues on.

See you later, and let it go.

Feel it and let it go.

Feel it and let it go.

The past is but a phantom seen, created by your imagination, that never was, and never will be, so let it go and exist within your eternal space now.

Live now.

You are wild.

You are wild happening to be only you,

And,

Live you now.

Live now.

You are alive now.

Put your invitations out without expectation, and simply continue to live.

Be what happens to you now.

There is nothing more to strive for, there is nothing more to gain.

*You are living with you, so please leave them.
They are all fine.*

Dad is filled with peace, and harmony, and goodness.

You are living now, and the more you let it all go, and live well, the more you will find that all is peace and love and goodness.

CLIMBING MT COUGAL

Climbing Mt Cougal.

*Trekking briskly the whole time
right along the edge of the NSW and Qld border
with a barbed wire fence next to me.*

Something about this metaphor.

Climbing, climbing.

*The only thing harder
than the heart thumping challenge of climbing up
is the slippery, life and limb risking*

descent.

SITTING NEXT TO MY FATHER

Sitting next to my father as he quietly lays there peacefully dozing, I wonder;

"What is all this?"

"What is a life?"

"What is life?"

And I can't grasp any of it.

I am not peaceful as he appears to be.

I am confused, and forced into a strained grasping at something that maybe is there, but is not of my present capacity to comprehend.

Perhaps we have everything back to front, and upside down.

Or perhaps it all just is, and we are part of it as is.

It's very lonely, and some other word I can't find to express the feelings/emotions, but it's something of emptiness like a small ship in the night sitting precariously on a vast endless ocean.

PINK BALLOON

A lone pink balloon bounces
away
off the sidewalk
and
into the path of the six lane highway.

It bounces,
and floats,
and is oblivious to
its imminent destruction,
and yet it continues to pop,
and bounce,
and float
and

never dies.

AND AS IT FADES FROM VIEW

*And as it fades from view
I signal to you
my forgiveness
and love*

*You gave me so much
I cannot recall
Everything*

Yet I know that it was good

*And there has been such pain
Amidst the beauty*

*For although I did not show it
I felt it all*

*And I loved it
And that is why it has been so hard
to go*

WE LEAVE THIS WORLD TO OTHERS

We leave this world to others
We leave this world to others
We leave this world to others

Whether we like it or not

We leave this world to others
We leave this world to others
We leave this world to others

Whether we like it or not

We leave this world to others
We leave this world to others

Leave this world to others

Whether you like it or not
everything you have ever loved, owned,

or desired
will be left to others

SOMETIMES

Sometimes it's just so painful

The past

The memories

The pain

I feel it in my gut...

and I wince.

FRAYED

My nerves are quite frayed around the edges from everything

But I continue on

I don't really have any choice

I look out over the beauteous cover of Jim the Roseman's roses and I am in awe

And yet there is a pain in the pit of my stomach

We continue to press on

We have no choice

Dad continues to suffer like nobody else and that's the worst of it

IN IT

When you're that close to someone, you're in it

There's no objectifying or anything then

There just is

You're in it,

and that's that

WHEN WAS THE LAST TIME

When was the last time we came up here for a game of cricket?

We didn't know it was going to be the last time,

but it was

the last time.

You,

standing there,

upright.

No miracle then.

It would be now.

Our last game of cricket.

Your last game of cricket.

Who knew?

We didn't.

Best we didn't.

We just enjoyed it.

Our last game of cricket.

Just like your last trip to the park with Lucy.

Lucy's passing, a forerunner to yours.

Bookended by B.

Oh how you would love to be back in those days.

Playing cricket.

Walking Lucy.

Being with B.

And that's where the pain comes.

Knowing what you would love.

And cannot have.

Ever again.

2 STONES GRINDING (TOGETHER)

2 old stones fallen from this mountain

grind hard.

The sound

of pure pain,

of loss beyond what can be spoken.

Intercontinental tectons,

weight dragging

you

from her,

as you

founder,

gasping.

She sits

reading.

She knows

your death,

even as this

breath,

gurgling,

keeps you

from your grave.

That sound

of a moraine

in creation

carves apart this love

to dust.

As, grinding,

stone upon stone,

nothing left,

not even bones,

ground down

ashes, rust,

leaving form,

becoming

us.

FINAL CALL

Undeserving of the pity

Undeserving of the grace

Just let me to sit a while

Taking in this place

Sitting by your bedside

Only at the end

The boat capsized

The captain drowned

Our ship awash with grief

Rapidly descending

We hear the final call
Letting go the tether

The snapping of the cord

AHH BUT DO NOT BE NAIVE

Ahh but do not be naive my dear Niel,

This traveller knows a few secrets.

The pain is concomitant with the pleasure.

The joy emerges from the seeds of sorrow.

What we do for others we do for ourselves.

Those who choose not to go will never see the entry sign.

DESCENT

At the counter this morning

Love greets me by name

Mary enquires

How am I today

I tell her the truth

Not easy to bear

Sitting, receptive

She's had worse to bear

She's carried it softly

From Syria here

And now she and Love

At the counter of care

She raises her hand

Betoking a gift

Her hand brings forth

The blessing I need

And as I depart from the counter of Love

I am blessed

While descending

the cool, dark

from above

HE WON'T BE LOOKING AT ANY OF THIS AGAIN

He won't be looking at any of this again from in that body.

It's tough,

And we will miss him and his ways.

We are all struggling.

He's done so well.

In those words of Paul in the bible;

"I have run the race,

I have fought the good fight."

Was that in Corinthians?

SATURDAY 14 DECEMBER

Awaking in the night

Standing

Encompassed by stars

Thinking of those who have passed

TOGETHER (EULOGY FOR DAD)

On the land where I live
a giant tree has fallen across the path.
It is huge. Way too big for any chainsaw.
What to do?
I can't go back,
but confronting its sheer immensity
it feels too much.
But the only way,
the ONLY way
is together.
To take the hand of my travelling companion,
and,
together,
to continue our journey.
Where once this giant stood
strong, and proud, and beautiful,
for years before we came here.
Now
We MUST
face this challenge,

and, in the aftermath
of this giant's death,
a gaping hole left in the forest,
new sunlight lighting our path,
we MUST
grasp this old giant's branches,
and together,
pushing and pulling each other,
climb upon this old giant.
This old giant becoming part of our path,
as he always was, as he sheltered us.
Now, having fallen
somehow touching us more intimately,
as parts of this old giant rub off on our hands, our boots.
As our hands, and knees, and shins are scraped, and out our
blood pours, merges with the crystalline sap of this old giant.
We have never been so close
as in this time, when the giant has fallen
into our hands.

DEATH

Death
It comes in and smashes everything

Incoming tide
Wipes clear all marks

Brickies trowel
Clean slate

Fucking hell
Bam!

All gone
All gone
All gone

47°C
ON 31 DECEMBER

It's so hot my eyes sting

I can feel the heat from the blasting wind peeling the skin off my face

It's ugly heat
Everything is hot to the touch

The car's outside temperature gauge reads 47°C

It's beyond sweat hot

FOR AULD LANG SYNE, MY DEAR

The time keeps passing.

We are in the last day, of the last year with Dad in his body.

And so, in some ways, to let go of this year is to let go of the time with Dad.

And letting go of the time with Dad is not easy.

So letting go of this year is hard.

This new year is our first year without having him the way that we had him for what seems like forever, and in some ways was.

But as the poet said:

*"no one can stop time's unfolding.
Never let go of the thread."[1]*

END OF THE DYING YEAR

The year ends

In a dry creek bed.

I find myself

Stationary.

Held within cicada force fields,

Burnt umber and sepia tones.

The rock, splintered.

Bitten, scratched and aching

I take the next step.

This year's bark

The ground that I now crunch.

I know the butterfly is here

Although I cannot see her.

And what hurts more,

She knows

But does not reveal.

Walking alone,

Fresh new shoots where the trunk came down.

And I have not been here

Since before this collapse.

And I am the tree.

And the shoots,

And it hurts,

As my fresh bark is exposed to 47 degree days.

The furnace burns all away,

Or almost,

For I remain.

Bereft.

HALF MOON

Half moon above

Half moon below

You struggled so hard

Ascent or decline

Your struggle

Valiant

As you climbed

Your feet dragging

Held by a thread

Diminishing

Struggling

From the bed

Collapsing

Slow motion

Gradually gone

Half moon

Becoming

Moon

Now gone

BROKEN BY THE TREE

So I leapt on that big old tree.

and I slipped,

and it threw me.

And as I lay on the ground,

for the first time in years

I heard the sound

of the fresh water flowing

. . .

from deep beneath the ground.

Wounded and broken,

and a little bit slowed,

I continue my journey

listening to the flow.

Water sprites guiding

I follow

down their path

below.

∼

We are but humble servants of powers we can't even begin to comprehend

∼

AT YOUR GRAVE

I'm staring at your grave

and I'm wearing your old shoes.

I'm staring at your grave

and I'm wearing your old shoes.

Worn, and broken, battered,

retrieved from that old bin.

All of this was yours,

there wasn't any sin.

I am yours still

as I come out 'cross your grave.

It's a bitter union junction.

It's the freedom of the slave.

I'm broken, and I'm tattered, I've fallen into that old bin.

Weeping from the heavens.

Emmanuel where've you been?

Emmanuel, Emmanuel, Emmanuel you've gone.

Emmanuel, Emmanuel,

Emmanuel, where you were seen.

Emmanuel it was your home but only for a time.

The ebony and ivory,

Nor was that a crime.

It's raining from the heavens as I pass by your old church.

It's raining from the heavens and I remember that old song.

I know you'll recognise her.

How does she bear it up?

I'm standing in your shoes

and I'm standing at your side.

Tidalik is laughing

'aint done that for so long.

So many times along this path, but never for this task.

I'm travelling to your grave site

even as I drive your car.

I'm standing in your shoes now,

and I am driving in your car.

All the kings horses and all the kings men could not put us back together again.

He's having eggs for breakfast,

and we are the menu.

You can be the entrée, I'll be following soon.

Heavens flood is not enough,

you didn't want to come here too.

All I can do is drive your car along this road anew.

I've had to push myself today,

couldn't ever do it before,

with temperatures so hot as that

I had to wait for more.

I'm standing in the rain now.

I'm standing in your shoes.

No way that I can fill 'em,

now I understand the blues.

John Lee, not mistaken

knew as much as you.

How on earth did we get here?

God I'm missing you.

Eyesight overtaken!

Eyesight overtaken!

God, I've got the blues.

And he is whisking omelette

just like you used to do.

It isn't any sacrilege.

It is our, "Oh Marg," to you.

That wasn't the joke I meant.

It's our homage to you.

But the joke is well received.

It's always been the way of you.

I'm looking at your shoes now.

Can't fit them like you do.

We are driving past McDonald's.

Do you remember too?

The shame came down one birthday.

I didn't know what to do.

We all have found our limits.

It makes us human too.

I know that you are freed now.

A freeman like the slave.

I'm leading the procession, way up to your grave.

I'm cold,

and oh so lonely.

With you it never was the case.

I'm broken and I'm shattered.

You should see my face.

Should I do this solo?

No, I'm not that brave.

I've planned to do it with him.

To visit at your grave.

The rain it keeps on falling,

as it always has,

but now you're a part of it,

and I am what they have.

I'm looking at your shoes now

before I put them on.

Blurry recognition,

what I am becoming.

And I can hardly bear it,

although you know I can.

I've come to ask your blessing,

something I already have.

I'm standing at your grave now

in this pouring rain.

It's not about the feelings,

it's about the man that you became.

Standing in the sunlight

with the family,

we said goodbye, or au revoir,

though it's not the same.

He taught me poetry,

he taught me how to write,

but in these shoes,

all wet right now,

I'm looking for a knife.

Because that's the only tool

that will do the job aright.

Searching through the blur,

stumbling in the night,

we sat in that old room.

It wasn't what it was.

Now I've gone and done it,

I've poured out what I could.

My blood upon your ground here,

sacrifices made.

You are now my Isaac.

Abraham is slayed.

I'm looking at your shoes now

as I put them on.

They're battered, and we're shattered,

and he hasn't come.

Monet's all I can think of.

A gift I found for you.

Just like our final visit

to our very own Louvre.

And that's where I took the photo.

It's where you took me too.

Treasures buried centuries,

revealed once with you.

And I'm waiting at your grave

beneath the pouring rain.

We're all waiting for someone.

Someone who never came.

I'm standing in your shoes.

I'm standing at your grave.

And we are smashed and broken.

But somehow we are okay.

The slave has found his freedom.

He has run away.

I caught a glimpse at Bondi

on that special day.

And though we're not together

in that original way,

we are still together

in the original way.

Waiting at your grave site,

wearing your old shoes.

He taught me poetry,

and now I've got the blues.

VISITS

I went to my Father's grave site,

but you know he wasn't there.

I went to my Father's graveside,

but you know he wasn't there.

I went to visit you where I thought you lay,

but you had gone and left that place,

nothing left to say,

You came upon Avanti

on another day.

We are grateful for your visit.

Won't you come again?

HAD YOU

I thought that I was ready
    And now I know I'm not
    They're calling from the bleachers
    & I am going on

Oh my God
    I tried so hard
    I tried so hard for you
    I'm sorry wasn't good enough
    I'm sorry were too few

We fought & tried
    And fell apart
    We fell apart a lot
    It had us on the run now
    It had us from the start

        . . .

And though we may be gone now
    And though we may be through
    Theres a feeling that's uncanny
    That's got a lot to do with you

They're calling from the bleachers
    I love you
    In this crowd
    I thought that I was ready
    Haven't got a lot

I hear them calling out your name
    I hear that sound a lot
    You reborn
    This body
    True

We gave in not a jot
    And though you're in that other world
    And I am here not you
    I feel you all around me
    And I'm grateful
    I had you

AND I REALLY FEEL YOU'RE GONE NOW

And I really feel you're gone now
Gone for oh so long

And I really feel your absence
And it's not a pleasant song

There are no words to say it
It's the measure that you're gone

We used to drive along here
You even spoke of moving on

But we never did believe it
We just played another song

Smell the flowers
Talked for hours

Didn't seem that wrong

You always were the driver
You didn't like to ride

Our chief and our commander
No one matched your stride

But you took that big bird out of here
Upon the steep ascent

You didn't leave us willingly
You fought till you were spent

And now we live in memory
Not forgotten not alone

We see you all around the place
We hold you close to home

WATCHING SEINFELD

We always loved the joke,

"Titleist?"

We would sit there in front of the TV, Dad in his large recliner, and me perched on the three seater.

We had a good laugh.

And then we would change channels over to the footy.

That's what we did.

. . .

I say we did that because, even though I have a lump in my throat, my not saying it doesn't change the fact that he has died.

And I only sat there in front of the TV to be there with him.

The joke was only funny when we watched it together.

The footy was only good when we watched it together.

I don't watch the TV now, nor do I sit there.

I leave his chair empty, and I get out of the house, and speak these words out.

I'm walking my own dog.
    She demands a lot.

Dad's dog's name was Lucy.
    My dog's name is grief.

SEARCHING FOR A COMPASS

*I'm not melancholy.
I'm just feeling into this.*

*This you not being around,
it's not a thing I've ever known.*

And now it's the only thing I know.

And it is territory uncharted.

*I'm searching for a compass.
I'm sure there's one around.*

*Searching for a compass,
amongst the unfound.*

*I'm searching for a compass
that once included you.*

Searching for a compass.

One that'll be just as true.

I'm searching for a compass.

Underneath all that,
I'm searching for my father
who held me just like that.

SUMMER...GONE

Summer's over.
You have gone.

I'm flying out,
Leaving our home.

Early mornings
Too much for me.

Waiting, hopeless
Eternity.

Car is running,
Shivering cold.

Now it's real,
You've really gone.

TELL ME WHY

We had some good times here together.
Though we didn't think we would.

I'm sad and I'm forlonging.
You and I we could.

And now I'm coming to you,
I am coming home.

So tell me why
I'm so lonely,
Tell me why I'm losing home.

LISTENING

Listening to Perfect,

And the tears come

As from the first.

Naught can be said;

It happened,

It was sad.

Still is

. . .

Perfect.

JERVIS BAY RECEDING

Jervis bay receding.
The river to the south.

Golden, slender
Lover.

Bursting at your mouth.

Staring at the sun,
to behold you
in full majesty.

Too much for anyone,
she's fleeting
on the shoreline;

waving,
waving,
waving.

On, and on,

Jervis bay receding.

My child,
Ready, gone.

Jervis bay receding.
Slender, golden brown.

Jervis bay receding.

Slow
candle
burning out.

Jervis bay receding.
The slender, and the brave.

Jervis bay receding.
If only for one day.

Jervis Bay
receding.

No more
do we go out.

A shifting,
fading shadow.
Figure with a hound.

MY NEW BOOT

My new boot is broken.
Just like that it blew.

And if I'm not mistaken.
It's a little bit like you.

Mobi-metronomey,
Leonard travelates.

Slowly going home,
and I am missing you.

Ask the strong man what to do,
'cause I haven't got a clue.

The strong man knows just what to do.

Clamp it up, and

weight it down,

then skip right out of town.

Upon the wing,
and on the road.

Doesn't matter how.

Strong man's knowing brings me heart.
So I prepare to start.

Strong man makes the way.

Folded up,
pressed right in.

Leave and go for days.

Just like him,
the Greyhound way.

Singing on the wind.

The fields lying fallow.
The strong man's making hay.

A stop,
a start,
a heart attack.

Waving me away.

I didn't know, forgive me sir,
your best
intended man.

He gave me love,
and all I did was spit upon his hand.

Another solo traveller upon this hardened ground.

We could go together, laughing with the crowd.

I didn't know,
I hadn't seen.

Forgive me now I pray.
For I have been a stranger
upon your right of way.

I thought I'd seen aright,
I thought I'd seen the way,

tearing at your Homeland
and your sovereigntay.

YOU HAVE TO GO WITH SOMETHING

You have to go with something more.

You have to go with that there is something more.

You have to go with that there is that something more,
that is that something more,
that is that something in you,
and in her.

You have to go with that something more.

That something, is this something more that is
calling you now even as you asked the question.

That something more is you.

And that something more is her.

So go with that.

Go with that something,

and go with that something more,
because that is the something more that is the
   something that is

the sum of you

and of her.

THIS ONE DARK NIGHT

All around the scents become me.

Maraya

intoxicating me.

White in this night.

Sounds of creatures
　　in the gloaming.

And I am a creature of this night.

Breeze wafting leaves.

Gardenia scents
where the branches browned and died out.

Beyond the light,
    and into the night.

Dark night love.
    Caressing my every limb.

Oh yeah,
    this,
    this night.

This one dark night
    of love,
    of warmth,
    of breezes coming.

Bringing me home
    to where you sat
    with Lucy
    in the light of the Sun.

ENDEAVOURING

We all go through different times in our lives.
    And that was a time that had to be gone through.

And now you are experiencing this time.

I have many changes happening.

Nicola will be driving herself by the end of September.

And obviously with Dad having passed my life has changed.

There is my art.
    And I'm grateful for this.

. . .

I do worry a bit about not having a formal source of income,
    but I also understand that we are part of something we don't understand.

So I'm endeavouring to relax and go with it,
    and to dance with the feelings of loss,
    and pain
    and longing,
    and allow these emotions to drive my artistic flow.

GIVING OVER

Giving over to mythology

Giving over to the truth

Giving over to the larger

Giving over to The Self

WHAT DO YOU DO?

*I'm looking out over the horizon,
waiting for the executioner to come.*

*But what if the executioner never comes?
What if nobody comes?
What then?*

Freedom?

*What do you do with your freedom?
What do you do with your time?
What do you do when you are alone?*

What do you do when you are alone with yourself?

What do you do when you are here?

What do you do if the executioner never comes?

Are you the executioner?

Or

are you your own begotten Saviour?

HORNS OF THE MOON

You are like a bull at a gate - always advancing.

Meander, and turn back on yourself.

Hers is monthly/moon calendar.

You are seeking a salve to your pain.

Learn to live with pain, with longing, with loss.

Be.

Learn to Be.

. . .

Love.

Gently move beyond anticipation.

HOW FOOLISH ARE WE?

One day we will be dead.

And then we will be a lot further apart than we are now.

So let us live while we can now before it is too late.

We have already lost ones that we love.

Are we so foolish that we would deny ourselves moments of beauty now while we can?

How foolish are we?

Hopefully not too foolish.

HIS ROSES

I have cut every single one of his roses
And placed them in a water jar.

Holding them close to my heart
I carry them to she who loved him.

The scent of the roses is the scent of him,

And it mixes with my sweat.
As I bend my back beneath the summer sun;

Each cut a memory,
Each rose a gift.

The gardener is gone.
The garden remains.

And I cut every single one of his roses
To bring to she who loved him.

*There is nothing else on this earth that I could give
    to her.*

*And tonight we will remember him,
Just as we had dined with him.*

*The scent of these roses
Mixes with my sweat,
And I'm okay with that.*

WAS THERE A TIME BEFORE THIS?

Was there a time before this?
    I can hardly remember the time before your diagnosis.
    And the actual time of the disease goes back even longer.

And so you struggled.
    And we struggled,

for longer than we feel we can remember,
    now wishing there was something we could have done.

But what?

I don't know,
    though this provides no comfort as the pain of the experience remains.

REVEILLE IN 3 PARTS

PART I

And at the end of the summer
there is water where there was none.

Much more water is coming
as the rains bear down upon us.

But much has been lost
and we remember the countless dead,

even as we gaze into this black pool,
unburning reflection of our world.

Dark heart pool.

Remembering
where we lay down,
begin again.

PART II

Weeping at this pool of reflection.
Incapable of speech.

I sweat this out.

I wish he were in his shoes.
Or at least I in his.

Or is this just a pool of vanity?

I did not speak his name,
let us just say Daffodil.

Gazing I see myself,
not entirely happy.

Hard rock grieving.

Even this pool cannot bear me up.

A trillion singing birds,
delighting,
bringing life
again, and again
to this cold stone.

Parsifal lying by the brook.
Heart stung lover
spying
the bridge that must be crossed.

Oh so dangerous.

And thrilling too.

*Each move
threatening doom.*

*Rising up.
Drawn to you.*

*Inevitable.
Together soon.*

*Laying down
intense light dawns
upon this broken rock.*

*These angels sing
their holy round
gathered in their wings.*

*The Honey Eater's flutter dance.
Aglow
Here with her mate.*

*Subtle song,
so gentle
brings,
the lover to her home.*

PART III

This light of love so strong that it even penetrates the greatest darkness.

I would not believe it had I not beheld it.

It has something to do with the peculiarities of the light.

The light has its own intelligence, and it brings it to me.

Gathering this light within I am transformed.

MARVELLING

*She said,
"Trust life",
at the spring of eternal water
upon return from my journey.*

*Nourishing me
with those birthday gifts
she said,
"Trust life",
diving beneath the water.*

*Marvelling
I followed
and she ministered to me.*

*Upon return from my journey
revealing her beauty, and her art,
a gift from the Indian sage.*

She said,

"Trust life".

We walked upon the skillion,
among the stars
she said,
"Trust life."

At the spring of eternal water;
her song,
her music,
her art,
nourishing me upon return from my journey.

PERPÉTUELLEMENT VERDOYANT

There is a strip of grass
Beneath the wall that has stayed green all summer
All the other grass is dead
Yet this strip has remained verdant
I do not understand it
Yet I love it all the same

THE SACRED WORD

> Be grateful for the gifts
> Each word sacred
> Do not abuse the gift
> Or Her
> Or Them

FROM A TIME WHEN YOU BOUNCED ME ON YOUR KNEE

Laid flat
   Upon this path

Looking up
   I see your Star

Brighter than you've ever been
   Reaching out to me again

The way you held me up
   So close

Loving eyes
   Dance-ing

. . .

I know your love
 From this one pic

LANDING

Landing this way
Last time
Mid Dec
Alone
Taking pics on Nikon he was still alive

WEST, AND FURTHER WEST

Dark
Step into the night wind

The rain
The pain
Doing what I must

Orion
With whom this journey began

West
And further west

Falling off the end of the earth

Where I melt
Into
You

DESIRING THAT

If summer were to go

And winter also

Then I would be happy

Without

Desiring

That which

Neither summer

Nor the winter bring

DEEP BEYOND

*The snake lays
beneath the clover.*

*Deep,
deep, beyond
any human calling.*

*As I stumble,
crying out
your name.*

*Penitent
to your saint,
longing for surrender.*

*Trudging
bootless calls.*

*Train never came,
cars too far.*

Desertion is my name.

*But I tried
to join her.*

Threw in all I had.

*While she
was
marching westward
I had other plans.*

*Up all night,
I missed the plan,
took in half the dark.*

*Saw the crow,
and turned around,
and sat upon the grass.*

*And as we cried
we heard the sounds
of people passing by.*

*Morning came,
and went again.*

*A stranger light
then came.*

*Closing doors,
shut up the shop,*

the carriage took us out,

far beyond the fields,
away from any house.

Shots rang out,
the only sound
wings flapping
'gainst the air.

The scent of dendrite powder
settling on my hair.

EVERY MAN MUST WALK

Every man must walk alone
    But

We can
    Hold hands

And carry
    On

4:30AM

4:30am
And I am
Unsleeping

The glow of the neighbouring farmhouse
Familiar
Warm

Out here
Wind
Buffets
My father's coat

The forest echoes
Crashing
Crashing
Down

Ancient forests
Crashing

To the ground

As frogs
Oblivious
Croak on

And the neighbouring farmhouse lights
Linger

BLESSED

                                        We who in her
                                          See our eyes

                                        Bless'd by Mary
                                          Sanctified

∽

After

When he was dying there was still dying left to be done

Now that he's died there's nothing

WHEN THE TASK HAS BEEN COMPLETED

*I had something to do
even though it wasn't pleasant,
or my choice.*

*It was
that thing to do,
and,
in the doing,
satisfying
pleasure
to be found.*

*Now,
my one desire
hampered
at the knees.*

*Awash with
grieving feelings,
not knowing who to be.*

*My case gone cold,
I'm stepping back
to who
is calling me.*

*A silent
call
I've heard before
in quiet
subtlety.*

WARMING SUN UPON MY FACE

Warming sun
Upon my face
As he loved so much

Lying
Dying
In his chair
Upon the Gracewood hutch

Sick bird
Nestled
Swaddled in
A child in her cot

We gave him all
We offered him
Gave him
All we've got

MY FATHER'S PASSING

My Father's passing
Becoming a not normal
Normal part of this life now

An unreal reality
A strange felt loss
An end that has happened
A loss that remains

Hollowed cavern
Like coming upon a nest
Fallen to the ground

That is what I feel
That is what I see

Thank you for walking
This with me

SEE YOU ON THE OTHER SIDE

I'm cleaning up

Their house
Their home
Their dream
Their lives

It's a messy business

Beginning and ending in darkness

Piercing pain
Memories, forgotten

You see the view
And
I feel much of the pain

Days wasted

Time
Gone

I'll see you
On the other side

WHEN I LEAVE

When I leave
all of your roses are bare

The light is coming in fast now beneath your
    luminescent man in the moon

But soon the man will be gone

May as well be to the other side of the world

Venus chases

Or is it the other way around?

I think it's both

And my stomach is a leaden balloon as I wait for the
    codeine and tryptophan to kick in

For we will party

Again and again
And again and again and again

Even as our shadows flicker
Possibly never to return
To this place

And yet,
Like the bush turkeys
We are still here

3 SISTERS

3 Sisters
Shrouded
Speak
Of dreaming
Time
Long
Going
On
And
Standing
Even as we rush
Home
They speak
Reminding me
They speak
We are here
We are still
Here
We remain
Here

I LEFT YOU

I left you
In the winter
Returning
In the spring
Knowing
You are changed
Mourning
All that's lost
Though I am not ready
Nothing I can do
The life bursting beyond me
Consuming all I knew
Holding on
And
Letting go
Doesn't stop the pain
Twisted gut
This loss is real
Closing out
My home

FACE CONTORTED

Face contorted
Memory
Each another stab
How much can I handle
How much to withstand
Each one cuts a little more
Until I'm all wrung out
Spurting
Bloody fountain
Less within now
Than without
Carried forth
Incapable
Of holding back the ride
All I ask
More time to breathe
To gather in my time

HERE AT THE HOUSE AT VINCENTIA

Here at the house at Vincentia
I can't quite touch this
Too close
So too far
Too much
And too many
Distracting
People
And so
I'm ghost walking
Not quite present
Not quite absent
On the lookout
And wary of Jan
The memories
Faded into a melange
I'm lost
Unable to
Go there
We do our things in a mad hurry

From one to the next
And this works well for me
Saves me from
The truth
Saves me from the pain
That's way too close
That I can't handle
Not today

WEEPING

On the Scribbly gum track
We weep
Together
As we discover
On this path
Together
Our lives
Sharing
Loss
And true mourning
The violet daffodil
Silently sings
A comfort
To our weeping

HER GRACE, SHE'S BRINGING

Climbing up my father's hill
I ask of her
And she replies
A little girl
A little girl
Is coming
Coming
She
Will live
This epoch through
Guided
Guiding
Gilded
Cup
Of waters sparkling
This
Divine
Coming now
Atop this hill

Her grace
She's bringing
A whole new world

LIVING LIGHT OF YOU

This is not what I saw
This is not the
EXPERIENCE!
Oh! If you could have been
Could have seen
THIS!
Magic so strong
It put me on the ground
Never before seen
As through these black trees
The whole of the light of life is seen
Startling
Like nothing else
She winks at me
This butterfly
As we
Enjoy
This spectacle
Which I wish you could have seen
A thousand radiant candles

Rising
Enfolding me
I think that's where you like to live
In fact I know it's true
A thousand radiant candles
Screened
A living light
Of you

ROCK

Slick wet rock
speaks to me
of Peter.

Stolid,
solid,
rock.

And
the rock remains,
but we
humans
being,
we go.

Leaving
each other,
we go
somewhere else.

Our marks fade,
as the creek carries us
further away
on that first
open sweep,
unaware
of our return.

LIGHT REVEALING

*I am stripping down,
I'm going bare,
can't hide myself
anymore.*

*Out here
I stand,
I cry.*

*I'm taking flight.
Giving
all I've got tonight.*

*Flint and stone,
let the sparks fly.*

*Ignite!
Ignite!*

Ignite the night sky!

BEAUTY'S GIFT

High summer
  Peacock feathers

Beauty's gift
  Fall

Lying
  At my feet

I bow
  Collecting each

Treasure
  Bunched against my heart

. . .

My heart's
 Glistening peacock feathers

Spread
 Before you

Delicate
 Wonders

At your feet

Beauty's gift
 Revealed

RECEIVING THE BLESSING

*And at that moment
when,
resolve failing,
reaching out
you dance your love,
and offer a gesture
orchestrating the heavens
with your love.*

*Clouds,
sacred moonlight
brightening to blinding.*

*In this beauty
you
gift to me
your blessing;
pure
strength,*

heart
to
proceed.

WHEN OLD SHELLS BREAK

Your suffering
Ended.
Finished,
Done.

Now a new beginning.

Do not weep for what you lost,
I continue being.

Form transformed
In beauty.

Living now
Anew.

When old shells break
We leave them,
To take another place.

So mourn our once togetherness,
Be sad for our lost belonging.

And,
Walk on through,
In beauty,
In the light
Of new sun's rays.

AND THEN I SAW

And then I saw those same curling mists
    I hadn't seen
    Since her birth.

Silver Sun's glare
    Above
    So below.

Movement in the depths,
    Stirring of my soul.

Bringing forth
    Into the World,

My newborn,
    A girl.

AFTER THE STORM HAS PASSED

Relieved
At the passing of the storm
I breathe.

Knowing more
Than I did
When I did grieve
Upon the shore
Of my forgetting.

And
An
Unbecoming hymn,
Taken
By the moonlight.

Thoughts
Of
Coming in.

MUSHROOM FLOWERS

Mushroom
Flowers
Here
Now
Life
Brings
Decay
If not from ashes
The least
Remains
Rise again
Skyward

TWO DUCKS

Two ducks swim
Side by side.

Silently
They swim

Across
Still water.

RETURNING TO THIS OLD GIANT
(TOGETHER AGAIN)

I rest upon her.

Soothing gentle rain
Upon my face.

And
I know
Ultimately
We won

A victory of sorts.

Not over that which cannot be defeated.

But,
Rather,
Ourselves,

As we sat there
Together,

As I do now,

With you here,

Soft, cooling rain upon my face.

And I realise,
This giant's falling,
Not an accident.
But an inevitability

Of life,
Presenting
A challenge
For us
To find

New growth
Together.

POSTSCRIPTUM

I once nursed a sick man
Who was dying for a year.

An initiation
For both of us.

His speech staccato,
Mine sadly inadequate.

But the books they helped.
I read to him

In amongst the tears.

Some days I was over it,
Others barely coped.

I once nursed a sick man
Who was dying for a year.

*We didn't know each week
If that would be his last.*

*We simply helped support him,
Helping with each task.*

*Incapable,
Slowing down,*

The wounded bull laid down,

*Unpleasant groanings
Were his only sound.*

*It came upon us quickly.
We were unprepared.*

*Unpeaceful in the quiet,
The suffering shouted out.*

*We no longer travelled,
Were lucky to go out.*

*Eventually he closed his eyes
Didn't make a sound.*

*The door was closed,
Lights turned out,*

And so I write this now.

NOTES

For Auld Lang Syne, My Dear

1. The Title of the poem "For Auld Lang Syne, My Dear" references the New Year's Eve poem of remembrance by the Scottish poet, Robert Burns. And the last lines are my own incorrect note from memory referencing the final lines of William Stafford's "The Way It Is" which my daughter read to Dad in the week before he passed.

ABOUT THE AUTHOR

SJP Dooley is a writer, voice artist, actor, photographer, & co-founder of Stellar Violets Life Library Living Museum & Gallery. Through these, and other avenues, he seeks to give voice to soul, and engage with what it means to be present on this earth at this time. Inside Out Heart emerged from the struggle that was the final chapter of his father's life.

Volume 1 Ebook ISBN: 978-1-922399-01-4

Volume 1 Paperback ISBN: 978-1-922399-00-7

Volume 1 Audiobook ISBN: 978-1-922399-03-8

www.stellarviolets.org

facebook.com/simon.dooley
twitter.com/simondooley
instagram.com/SJPDooley

ALSO BY SJP DOOLEY

Inside Out Heart Volume 2: Diary notes of being with my dying father

Inside Out Heart Collection: Volumes 1 & 2

Inside Out Heart spoken word poetry to music by SJP Dooley & Paul Avanti Iannuzzelli

www.ingramcontent.com/pod-product-compliance
Lightning Source LLC
Chambersburg PA
CBHW071732080526
44588CB00013B/1999